# Beginning Tennis

## REVISED EDITION

## Peter Everett
*Florida State University*

## Virginia Dumas Skillman
*formerly Florida State University*

D0724015

*Wadsworth Publishing Company, Inc.*
*Belmont, California*

teach GV995.E9.1968

Illustrations by Marie Nava

4 5 6 7 8 9 10–74 73 72 71

L.C. Cat. Card No.: 68–25413

Printed in the United States of America

# Contents

# VALUES

Any worthy sport demands a degree of skill that can be obtained through practice and determination; it requires such muscular power and agility that a person must train to be at his best; it involves mental alertness for developing strategy; it demands sportsmanship and character; it offers keen competition and a thrill to the player as well as to the spectator; and, finally, it provides enough physical stress to help fulfill a person's need for exercise.

Tennis is such a sport. It is inexpensive and suitable to all age groups, to people of varying levels of skill, and to either sex, separately or together. To be a topnotch player requires much practice; on the other hand, an average player can obtain enough skill to derive immense enjoyment from the game. This versatility has made tennis a universal sport.

The universality of the game overcomes language barriers between people of different nations. And there is no special social class in tennis —you are a "tennis player," and differences exist only in level of competition. Friendships are also enhanced through play on the courts. The fact that two can play makes it easy to arrange a time for tennis.

Tennis offers a physical challenge for almost everyone. It brings to the busy person a good, quick form of exercise in a most enjoyable setting. It does not require a high degree of strength, but it can require a level of endurance comparable to that of any other sport. Endurance, speed, and agility can compensate for size. But tennis is not all physical. The mind must determine the opponent's weaknesses and his line of strategy, and set up a plan to offset his attack. Good playing requires more than good shots; many matches are won or lost on the basis of strategy alone.

In any competition, in front of the largest or smallest of audiences, the real thrill of tennis is the challenge of outplaying the opponent. An exciting and exhilarating feeling possesses you after a good shot or play; and there is no greater challenge than that which lies before the player who has just been outplayed by his opponent as he vows to work harder so that he can become better and try it again.

# HISTORY

The game referred to in the United States as *tennis* should rightfully be called *lawn tennis*. The true game of tennis is played in a walled and roofed court, with a racket larger than the lawn tennis racket, and with a ball made of tightly wound strips of cloth tied with twine, then wound with twine and covered with melton cloth.

In the ball games of the Greeks and the Romans, rudiments of the French game *jeu de paume* have been detected. *Jeu de paume*, similar to present-day tennis, was played as early as 1300. First played with the hands, it soon evolved into a game played with rackets. During the sixteenth and seventeenth centuries it was very popular in England and France, but during the eighteenth century a gradual decline started, and by the nineteenth century only the wealthy were playing. The word "tennis" was probably derived from the French term *tenez*, which means "Take it! Play!"

Lawn tennis was originated by Major Walter Clopton Wingfield in England in 1873. He combined aspects of racquets, badminton, and court tennis to obtain the game he first called "Sphairistike." This name was soon changed to lawn tennis because of its being played on lawns and its close resemblance to tennis. The first court was in the shape of an hourglass with a net 7 feet high across the center. In 1874 Major Wingfield patented a portable court and net, but due to public demands he freed the game for popular use in 1875. The All England Croquet Club at Wimbledon then devoted some of their lawns to the new game in hopes of pulling themselves out of financial difficulty. In 1877 they held their first world amateur championship tournament, which is now the famous Wimbledon Tournament.

Lawn tennis was brought to the United States in 1874 by Miss Mary Ewing Outerbridge after a vacation in Bermuda, where the game had been introduced by an army friend of Major Wingfield's. The first lawn tennis tournament in the United States was held at Nahant in August 1876. In May 1881, a convention was called to settle the confusion over differences in rules, size and weight of the ball, height of the net, and the system of scoring. An outcome of the meeting was the organization of the United States National Lawn Tennis Association. ("National" was dropped from the title in 1920.) Dr. James Dwight, often referred to as the "Father of American Tennis," was president of the Association for twenty-one years.

In 1900 Dwight Davis, inventor of the American twist service, donated a cup which bears his name for an international match between the United States and England. Out of this competition has grown a world-wide championship, and the Davis Cup is now the emblem of world amateur team championship. Competition for the Davis Cup is divided into zones—American, European, and Eastern. Countries that are interested may enter an elimination process in one of these zones.

Mrs. George Wightman, who was a national singles champion in the United States for several years, put up an international trophy known as the Wightman Cup for a woman's team match between the United States and England in 1923. The International Lawn Tennis Federation inaugurated broader international team competition for women in 1962 entitled the Federation Cup. It provides a single elimination tournament for teams based on two singles and one doubles match.

Amateur tournament competition is also very prominent in many countries. The most famous of these is Wimbledon in England, where the world championships are held. Another outstanding tournament is the United States' National Tournament at Forest Hills, Long Island.

The growth of tennis is being greatly stimulated by cooperation between the United States Lawn Tennis Association and the American Association for Health, Physical Education, and Recreation in promoting a Junior Development Program within the schools and communities throughout the country and by the Lifetime Sports Education Project, which is conducting clinics for teachers.

# EQUIPMENT

## BALL

Tennis balls are made from wool felt and natural, synthetic, or cold rubber. The rubber is molded into two cups, which are cemented together and covered with the felt. The hollow inside of the ball is inflated with compressed air or gas. Nonpressurized balls are manufactured that get their bounce from the rubber. The official rules of the United States Lawn Tennis Association include specifications for an official ball. Manufacturers who follow these specifications will stamp "Approved by the USLTA" on the ball or the package in which it comes. This means that at the time the ball was packed, it met the required specifications. At a later date, however, this may not be true because the pressure of the compressed air or gas in the ball will decrease and cause the ball to lose some of its bounce. Balls packed in airtight cans maintain the original specifications for six to eight months, while balls packed in other types of packages maintain specifications for a much shorter period of time—six to eight weeks. Balls that do not meet specifications are referred to as "seconds" and may be purchased at a lower price. Other factors influencing the cost of tennis balls are the quality of felt used and the type of container in which they are packed. (Airtight cans are more expensive than other types of packages.)

## RACKET

The present-day racket consists of many high-grade pieces of wood skillfully put together with the aid of glue, pressure, and heat. The frame of the racket is made of laminated (plied) strips of ash and fiber molded to form what appears to be one continuous piece of wood. The outside strip of the frame is often composed of a hardwood to make it more durable. The throat of the racket is made with hardwood also; maple or beech is most commonly used. The grip is made of basswood or Malacca and covered with leather, plastic, rubber, or imitation leather. The better rackets use leather.

The racket is strung with gut or nylon. Gut is used in the better rackets and is preferred by highly skilled players because of its resiliency (snap or spring). Gut is more expensive than nylon and is not moisture-proof. Dampness tends to increase the tension of the string, and

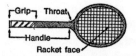

*Illustration 1—Tennis racket*

continued contact with moisture can cause the strings to swell to the breaking point. Nylon is moistureproof, but because of its elastic qualities it presents problems in maintaining proper tension. For the average player, however, it gives good service and is reasonable in cost. For regular play, fifteen-gauge tennis strings are used. For tournament play, sixteen-gauge string is usually used, but some players prefer seventeen-gauge. Seventeen-gauge is the thinnest, with the highest degree of resiliency but the least durability. The tension used when stringing a racket is from 50 to 60 pounds for the average player and up to 70 pounds for the highly skilled player. The degree of tension is usually determined by personal preference. Since high tension makes it difficult to control shots, tension should be increased only to the point where maximum accuracy can be maintained.

Rackets come in various weights and grip sizes. For best results, a racket should fit comfortably in the hand and be of a weight that is easily handled. Rackets are made in three weight categories—light, medium, and heavy—with a range in weight from 12½ to 14¾ ounces. Women usually choose a racket weighing from 12½ to 13¾ ounces, while men choose one weighing from 13½ to 14¾ ounces. Rackets that are too heavy cause undue fatigue and faulty stroking. Rackets that are too light hinder good control, because more force is exerted on the ball by means of the swing rather than by the racket itself. Grip sizes vary from 4½ to 5 inches, with women selecting a grip ranging from 4½ to 4¾ inches, and men choosing a grip from 4⅝ to 5 inches. Handles that seem easy to hold because they are small tend to twist on contact with the ball.

Another factor is racket balance. A racket may be head heavy, handle heavy, or evenly balanced. Persons who play a base line game usually prefer a head heavy racket, while persons who play a net game usually prefer an even balance or one with the handle heavy.

## NET

Nets are constructed of hemp, cotton cord, nylon, or metal. Metal nets cost more than cord nets, but they also last longer. Cord nets come in different sized threads with the more expensive nets having the larger diameter thread. High-quality nets are reinforced in the center section with more twine to withstand the added beating of the balls that fail to go over the net. Nets used out-of-doors should be coated with tar to give them better weathering properties.

## DRESS

The costume of the tennis player is white. It is proper for all tournament players, and the only exception comes in informal play. Women wear a shirt-and-short combination or a tennis dress. Men wear a one-quarter sleeve knit sport shirt and shorts or slacks. Shorts are usually of medium length for both men and women. Shoes should be flat, both soles and heels, with canvas uppers and rubber soles. The soles should not have large perforations that may damage the surface of the court. Socks should be medium or heavyweight wool or nylon composition to be absorbent.

*Illustration 2*    *Illustration 3*

## CARE OF EQUIPMENT

1. Keep racket in a press with equal pressure on all screws. Lay it on a flat surface or support it by the throat on brackets.
2. Keep racket in a waterproof case.
3. Do not use the racket to hit objects other than a tennis ball. Do not roll or scrape the racket along the ground to pick up balls.
4. Dry the racket with a cloth after it has been wet and rub the end

of a candle over the strings to keep them from drying out too quickly and snapping.

5. Wax the frame periodically to preserve the wood, and shellac the strings to protect them. Varnish the frame if it becomes worn.

6. Do not lay the racket where it may be stepped on.

7. Keep equipment at temperatures that avoid extremes of hot and cold.

8. Replace balls that become wet; dampness harms the stringing.

9. Slacken the net cable when the net is not in use.

10. Repair any net damage immediately, while it is small.

# TECHNIQUES
# OF PARTICIPATION

## THE GAME

There are two separate games of tennis, singles and doubles. The singles game is played by two players on opposite sides of the net on a court 78 feet long and 27 feet wide. The server first stands behind the

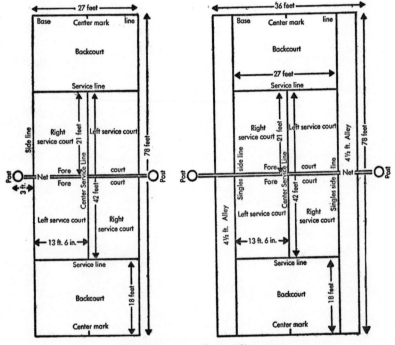

*Illustration 4—Court diagrams*

base line to the right of the center mark and has two tries to put the ball into play by throwing the ball up and striking it into the opponent's right-hand service court. The receiver returns the ball after its first bounce, and thereafter play consists of hitting the ball back and forth across the net until either side fails to make a good return. After the first point, the server stands behind the base line to the left of the center mark and serves into the opponent's left-hand service court. Thereafter the server alternates serving into the right- and left-hand service courts until the game is completed, whereupon the server becomes the receiver and the receiver, the server.

The doubles game is played by four people, two partners on each side of the net. In doubles, each player of a team serves a game in his turn, followed by a server of the opposing team, the serve alternating in the same order throughout a set. The game is played as in singles, and either partner of a team may hit the ball during play.

## FUNDAMENTALS

### GRIPS

There are three kinds of grips: the Eastern, the Western, and the Continental. The *Eastern Grip* is the one most widely used and taught because of its efficiency in executing the strokes in tennis. The Eastern forehand grip is often referred to as the "shake hands" grip; the racket is placed on edge, racket face perpendicular to the ground, and then the racket handle is grasped as if the player were shaking hands with it. The hand is placed so that the heel is against the leather butt at the end of the handle, and the fingers are spread along the handle with the forefinger extended farther up to ensure better grip and control. The thumb and index finger should make a "V" just slightly to the left of

*Illustration 5—Forehand grip*     *Illustration 6—Backhand grip*

center on top of the grip (Illus. 5). The backhand grip is obtained by moving the hand approximately a quarter of a turn counterclockwise from the Eastern forehand position so that the "V" between the thumb and forefinger is at the inner edge of the handle, and the thumb is straight or diagonally across the back side of the handle (Illus. 6).

The *Continental Grip* involves shifting the hand a quarter of a turn counterclockwise of the Eastern forehand, so that it assumes the same grip as the Eastern backhand when the thumb is in a diagonal position. It is not a desirable grip because of the strain on the forearm muscles and its ineffectiveness in handling high-bouncing balls.

The *Western Grip* is obtained by laying the racket flat and simply picking it up. It is used very seldom today because of the difficulty in executing low shots and volleys.

## READY POSITION

The ready position is the stance assumed while waiting to receive a serve or to return balls during play. Use the following position in preparing to return either low or high shots:

    1. hold racket lightly and directly in front of you;

    2. use forehand grip with racket held by throat in left hand;

    3. face net, spread feet with weight evenly distributed, and bend legs and back slightly.

*Illustration 7—Ready position*

### Where to Stand When Receiving Service

There is really no set position for receiving the service. The type and strength of the opponent's serve and the status of the receiver's own skills and reflexes help determine the exact receiving position.

Generally speaking, however, the recommended position for receiving in both service courts is about a foot inside the singles side lines and close to the base line. For fast, high-bouncing serves, a position just behind the base line or farther back is desirable. Slower, low-bouncing balls can best be handled directly in front of the base line, or closer if the serve is quite weak.

A common fault of beginners is to stand too far to one side of either service area to protect a weak forehand or backhand. An opponent

with placement and speed can wreck this defense by serving a fast ball
to the unprotected side.

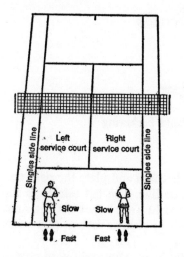
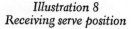

*Illustration 8*
*Receiving serve position*

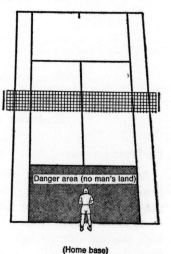

*Illustration 9*
*Playing position*

### Where to Stand during Play

For base line play, the best position is about two or three feet behind
the base line in the center of the court. With this position as "home
base," the player can move effectively from side to side or up and back.
After each return from the backcourt, you should immediately go
to home base, so as to be in position for the next return. When retrieving a ball hit into the forecourt, you will more than likely choose
to follow it up to the net rather than to return to home base.

## THE STROKES

### Forehand Drive

The forehand drive, executed on the right-hand side of the body (all
descriptions are for right-handed players), is the shot most often used
in tennis. A good forehand drive is a basic fundamental in becoming
a topflight player and in playing a truly effective game of tennis. Three
essentials in the forehand stroke are (1) backswing, (2) contact with
the ball, and (3) follow-through.

*Illustration 10—Forehand backswing*

### Backswing

As the ball approaches, pivot on the left foot and place the right foot behind the body so that it faces the side line. The left side faces the net, and the body weight shifts to the right (rear) foot. At the same time, move the racket back in a straight or circular motion to a waist-high position directly behind the right hip. This movement is made from the shoulder with the arm slightly bent. The ready position can be likened to standing in the middle of a clock with the racket pointing straight ahead toward twelve o'clock. To execute the backswing, swing the racket in an arc past three o'clock to six o'clock with the racket face perpendicular to the ground.

### Contact with the Ball

Stepping diagonally forward with the left (forward) foot so that the weight is transferred from the back foot to the front foot, swing the racket in an arc from the six o'clock toward the three o'clock position. The racket is in a position parallel to the ground, with the face flat as it meets the ball slightly in front of the forward foot. At the instant of

*Illustration 11—Forehand contact*

contact fully extend your arm with the wrist and grip tight to prevent the racket from turning in your hand. For an effective shot, attempt to hit the ball about waist high. If the ball is below the waist, bend the knees to bring the waist down to the level of the ball. But if the ball bounces above waist level, move back to allow the ball to drop to the proper height. In most cases the ball should be contacted at the peak of its bounce.

### Follow-through

As the racket hits the ball, it begins to come around the far side of the ball, forward toward the net, and then slightly up and around. The arm bends naturally, and the upward movement gives the necessary lift to the ball to direct it over the net. In order to get maximum power and efficiency, the shoulders turn to follow the direction of the racket, and the body weight is forward over the left foot. The right (rear) foot stays behind to serve as a balancer and to insure proper weight transfer.

*Illustration 12—Forehand follow-through*

For best stroke production you should feel that the racket is an extension of your arm. The follow-through adds continuity to the stroke, helping to assure proper speed and direction at contact.

#### Backhand Drive

The backhand drive is made on the left-hand side of the body. Many authorities contend that this is more natural and easier than the forehand, since you do not have to hit across the body.

In the backhand grip, move your hand to the left about a quarter of a turn, so that the heel of the hand rests on top of the handle. This position is necessary in order to hit the ball with a flat racket face, and to allow for more power and control of the shot. Change to this grip as you begin your backswing with the left hand holding the throat of the racket. Although this may seem difficult, with practice it becomes automatic.

### Backswing

From the ready position pivot on the right foot and place the left foot behind the body in a position parallel to the net. Face the net with the right side, and shift the body weight to the left (rear) foot. The body should turn well around so that it will not be in the way, allowing a free, unrestricted swing. Simultaneously, bring the racket back in a straight or circular motion guided by the left hand at the throat of the racket, so that it comes to a position behind the left hip. Here again the movement is from the shoulder, with the arm slightly bent and

*Illustration 13—Backhand backswing*

farther out from the body than in the forehand stroke, in order to give more power and freedom in executing the shot. The shoulders are swung well around to the left for increased power, and the feet are approximately parallel and spread comfortably apart, toes toward the side line.

### Contact with the Ball

On the forward swing the racket travels out and away from the body toward the nine o'clock position as you step diagonally forward and transfer your weight from the left (back) to the right (forward) foot. Contact the ball slightly in front of your forward foot, waist high, with a flat-faced racket in a position parallel to the ground. Your arm is fully extended at contact point with the wrist and grip held firm.

*Illustration 14—Backhand contact*

## Follow-through

The arm movement continues straight forward toward the net, and then turns slightly up and around with a free, easy motion out and away from the body. Swing the racket in the direction you intend the ball to go, as you transfer your weight to the right (forward) foot. The left (rear) foot serves as a balancer and ensures proper weight transfer. Pivot your shoulders and hips to give added power and to help swing the racket around your body for upward lift and topspin to the ball.

*Illustration 15—Backhand follow-through*

### Importance of Developing the Backhand

Having a good backhand is important because most players direct their serves to the backhand side and concentrate their shots where they consider the opponent to be weakest. Nothing can be more damaging to your confidence than to have an opponent hammer away at a weak backhand that becomes weaker as play continues. Most beginners with weak backhands have a tendency to run around them and use the forehand instead. This is not at all satisfactory because of the lack of time and the impossible task of maintaining proper position and balance. Each shot that goes to the backhand side should be hit using the backhand stroke.

### Tips on Forehand and Backhand Techniques

1. Bend the knees and shift the weight to the forward foot in executing either the forehand or the backhand stroke.

2. Use a full backswing to get a complete pivot, ensuring greater speed and control. However, an exaggerated backswing is not desirable because of the amount of time involved.

3. Keep your eyes on the ball at all times and follow through in the direction in which you intend the ball to go.

4. Hit the ball about waist high because this is the most natural position and the one from which the greatest amount of power and accuracy can be obtained. Balls played below the waist must be hit up, resulting in loss of speed, and shoulder height balls are awkward and difficult to play with accuracy.

5. Hit the ball using a flat stroke rather than a chop or spin stroke because a spinning ball is slow in flight, and the greater the angle involved, the greater the chance for error and loss of control. Also, it takes a greater amount of energy to impart spin to the ball and is hardly worth the quick exhaustion it brings. Top-ranking players use spin only occasionally as the situation demands to change the pace of the ball and to keep the opponent guessing.

6. Hit the ball at the height of its bounce because:

   a. You can thereby make use of the pace imparted to the ball by your opponent.

   b. Your opponent has less time to recover from the previous shot.

   c. You can reach the net position sooner.

7. Execute the forehand and backhand strokes as follows:

   a. Decide as ball leaves opponent's racket to use forehand or backhand.

   b. Swing racket to appropriate side.

   c. Pivot body and feet into proper position with short skips or bounces.

   d. Shift weight and start racket forward as ball bounces.

e. Contact ball at proper height and uncoil body to impart pace to arm and racket.

f. Maintain contact through hitting area (pretend ball is long and racket must go through its length).

g. Complete shift of weight and follow through with racket in direction in which the ball is intended to go.

h. Return to waiting position at center of base line.

8. Learn both the forehand and backhand strokes by using the following progression:

a. Practice swinging the racket correctly.

b. Hit a dropped ball.

c. Hit a tossed ball.

d. Run to hit a tossed ball.

e. Rally the ball.

## THE IMPORTANCE OF GOOD FOOTWORK

A prime requisite for success in tennis, as in other sports, is proper footwork. A perfect racket swing means little when you are too close to the ball, or when you fail to anticipate and keep your weight forward, ready to move into the ball. Perfect timing can compensate to some degree for faulty footwork, but few persons have such a sense of timing. Even good timing does little to make up for loss of body power or accuracy if the weight is on the wrong foot.

When the ball is several steps away, approach it with short steps. In running for balls at a greater distance, run quickly to the position where you think you should stop, and get set for the ball. A "skip-step" or a "two-step" is often used to get into the proper stroking position.

Good footwork is important in supplementing the arm swing to ensure greater power and balance and in determining the direction of the shot. When hitting a cross-court forehand, for example, place the left foot and leg more toward that direction for better stroke production, although it is wise to conceal shot direction as much as possible. The opponent can often determine the direction of your return by observing the placement of your feet. Keeping your weight forward on the balls of your feet while being quick to anticipate and go after your opponent's shot can make the difference in a close tennis match.

### THE SERVE

The serve puts the ball into play and can be a particularly strong offensive weapon. In today's fast play, the "big serve" has become increasingly important and is a great advantage to those who have developed it.

#### Types of Serves

The three types of serves are (1) flat or cannonball, (2) slice, and (3) American twist. The basic motion in all types is that of throwing a ball overarm. Although outstanding players may use all three types of serves as the situation demands, it is advisable for the beginner to learn the fundamentals of either the flat or the slice service.

#### Flat or Cannonball

This serve, hit with a flat racket face, is usually intended as a hard, fast, first serve. Throw the ball up slightly to the right of your forward shoulder and to a height above the full extension of your arm and racket. (Illus. 16.)

#### Slice

Sidespin from right to left is given to the ball in this serve. The ball is thrown more to the right than in the flat serve, and the arm and racket do not reach full extension at contact. The serve curves toward the right side of the opponent's service court. (Illus. 17.)

*Illustration 16*
*Flat serve*

*Illustration 17*
*Slice serve*

*Illustration 18*
*American twist serve*

*American Twist*

The spin on the ball is from left to right. Throw the ball more to the left than in the flat serve and slightly over the head. The ball bounces high and curves sharply to the left. This is by far the most difficult type of serve to learn and is executed by more advanced players. (Illus. 18.)

### Grip

For beginners the service grip usually recommended is the same as the Eastern forehand, which allows for a flat stroke. More advanced players usually prefer a grip between the Eastern forehand and backhand positions, which imparts more spin to the ball.

### Service Stance

1. Place your feet comfortably apart, with weight evenly distributed several inches behind the base line.

2. Turn slightly sideways (about a 45-degree angle) so that your forward shoulder points in the direction of the desired service court. This sideways position allows for more power and spin on the serve.

3. Point the racket straight toward the net and support it by the left hand holding the balls.

*Illustration 19*
*Service stance*

*Illustration 20*
*Service backswing*

### Service Backswing

From the starting position drop your racket straight down in a pendulum motion. As the racket arm passes your rear leg, open the wrist and racket face outward, continuing an upward swing until the racket arm is in a position similar to the forehand backswing position. At this point bend the arm, bringing the racket head up and dropping it behind your back in a "back-scratching position." At the same time transfer your weight to your rear foot, and arch your back. As you begin the backswing, fully extend the left arm upward, tossing the ball slightly to the right of the forward shoulder so that it goes somewhat higher than the right arm and racket in a fully extended position.

### Service Point of Contact

Reach straight up with the racket arm so that it is fully extended and contacts the ball near the beginning of the descent of the ball. As the racket makes contact, snap your wrist forward and down to give the ball power and descent into the proper service court. Simultaneously, bring the body around and forward into the stroke, transferring the weight from the rear to the forward foot.

### Service Follow-through

The racket arm continues its forward motion toward the proper service court, downward across the forward leg and around the body

*Illustration 21*
*Service contact*

*Illustration 22*
*Service follow-through*

with a free, unchecked swing. Bring the back shoulder forward so that the full weight of the body goes into the shot. More advanced players swing the right foot forward and across the base line for additional force and power.

### Where to Stand When Serving

Generally speaking, while serving in singles play, take a position close to the center of the court. When serving into the right service court (X in Illus. 23), stand slightly to the right of the center mark. When serving into the left service court (Y in Illus. 23), however, the best position is about 3 feet to the left of the center mark. This farther position gives a sharper angle when serving to the opponent's backhand. In doubles, assume a position slightly farther from the center mark for both service courts, since you have to cover a greater area than in singles play. However, some authorities recommend that, when serving into the right service court, the singles service position will make a better placement to the receiver's backhand.

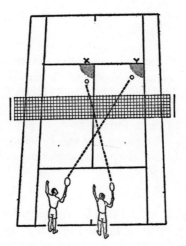

*Illustration 23—Service positions*

### Service Strategy

1. Make sure the opponent is ready before serving. Always have two

balls in the hand before beginning the serve.

2. Keep both feet behind the base line until after you have hit the ball.

3. Develop a consistent toss. A good swing means little when balls are tossed too high, too low, or too far to the front, back, or sides.

4. Keep your eyes on the ball constantly. Timing is especially important when serving.

5. Try to make the first service good, and do not serve "double faults." It is not a good policy to give away points.

6. Develop a serve with moderate pace and speed. Placement and accuracy come first; power comes later.

7. Develop a dependable second service. A slice serve with some spin would be effective. The full stroke should be the same as for the first serve.

8. Aim to the opponent's weakness, but vary placements to prevent his getting set for the shot.

9. Serve deep into the service areas, usually at angles, but occasionally straight at the opponent.

10. Vary the speed, spin, and placement of the ball to keep the receiver guessing.

## THE VOLLEY

The volley is used primarily near the net to hit a ball before it bounces. This is an offensive shot, and it may be executed on either the forehand or the backhand side. Good players find this shot a great advantage in "putting the ball away" after gaining the net position. Advance to the net with deep, forcing shots to put the opponent on the defensive. From this net position you can handle your opponent's weak return by volleying the ball deep or at angles out of his reach.

### Where to Stand

In singles, the usual net position is on the center service line, a little closer than midway between the net and the service line. With this position as home base, shift to the right or left as necessary to cover either service court area (Illus. 24).

In the doubles game, the net position for either the right or left service court area is the same in relation to the net and service line but is midway between the center service line and the doubles side line (Illus. 25).

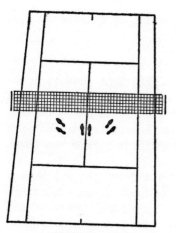

*Illustration 24*
*Singles net position*

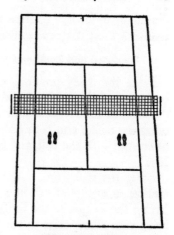

*Illustration 25*
*Doubles net position*

### Grip

The usual grips for the forehand and backhand volleys are the same as those used when making drives. Some authorities recommend using the Continental grip because often there is little time for changing the grip from the forehand to the backhand position.

### Body Stance

Footwork is as important in the production of the volley as it is in executing forehand and backhand strokes. However, time does not always permit a full sideward turn when making a volley. Although you

*Illustration 26*
*Volley backswing*

*Illustration 27*
*Volley contact*

should strive for this position whenever possible, many times you must assume a more diagonal stance.

### Forehand and Backhand Volleys

From the ready position, with knees slightly bent, pivot as in the beginning of the forehand and backhand swings. Cock the wrist so that the head of the racket is well above wrist level. Before hitting the ball, bring the racket arm back only about a foot behind the intended point of contact with the ball, and transfer the weight to the rear foot (Illus. 26).

Bring the racket-arm toward the net in a downward and forward motion to meet the ball at a point well in front of you, while transferring the weight to the forward foot. At contact lock your wrist, and bring your elbow close to your body. The volley is more of a "punch" than a full stroke, with a minimum of backswing and follow-through (Illus. 27).

Follow through about a foot or two in front of you with the racket pointed in the direction in which you intend the ball to go (Illus. 28).

The ideal volley is made at shoulder height. On a low shot, bend down to the ball, and tilt the racket back. The lower the ball, the more open the racket face has to be to send the ball over the net. Never drop the racket head below wrist level. Hit the volley flat rather than with spin so as not to slow it down.

### Placement of the Volley

The volley should be a "putaway" shot, since it is easy to be put on the defensive and lose the point if the volley is not a winner. This shot is usually directed away from the opponent with either a hard, fast, deep shot, or with a slower, sharply angled shot. Sometimes a "stop-volley" is employed, a blocked shot barely dropping over the net, which is almost a sure point winner if successful. In doubles, a hard, low shot

*Illustration 28—Volley follow-through*

hit deep in the middle of the opponents' court is most effective, since both opponents are caught off guard, not knowing soon enough which partner should attempt the return.

## THE HALF-VOLLEY

This is a "pickup" shot made about mid-court by a player out of proper net position. The ball is hit immediately after it bounces with a stiff arm and wrist block, and the body is bent well down toward the level of the ball. There is practically no backswing or follow-through, and the racket tilts slightly upward to direct the ball over the net. Although it is a defensive shot, the stroke can be made effective by proper placement of the ball (Illus. 29, 30, 31).

*Illustration 29* | *Illustration 30* | *Illustration 31*
*Forehand half-volley* | *Forehand half-volley* | *Forehand half-volley*
*backswing* | *contact* | *follow-through*

## THE LOB

The lob is a soft, high shot directed over the opponent's head deep into the backcourt. It is usually a defensive shot, to force an opponent to vacate the net position or to allow you more time to get back into position after being forced out of court. The lob may be used offensively when your opponent is close to the net, and when the lob has a safe minimum of loft, some topspin, and good placement.

The grip is the same as for the forehand or the backhand drive. There is very little backswing, the racket head tilts upward at contact with the ball, and the racket arm continues slightly upward, sending the ball high into the air. The lob may also be executed with a great deal of wrist action and practically no follow-through when you have little time and are out of position (Illus. 32, 33, 34).

Illustration 32
Forehand lob
backswing

Illustration 33
Forehand lob
contact

Illustration 34
Forehand lob
follow-through

## THE OVERHEAD SMASH

This stroke, usually made from the net position, is the reply to the lob, and is intended as an outright point winner. The grip and motion in executing the smash are like those of the serve. The player should make the backswing while getting into proper position to hit the smash, and the ball should be contacted at a point slightly farther in front of the body in order to give it a more downward trajectory. Some of the better players jump high into the air to meet the ball, adding height advantage. Since it is necessary, but often difficult, to achieve good timing in smashing a ball traveling through the air, it is desirable many times to allow the ball to bounce first before executing the smash.

Hit the ball at a hard and fast pace away from your opponent. It is best to hit the ball deep unless an angle shot is used. After making the shot, regain the net position, if not already there, in case the smash fails to be an immediate point winner. Sometimes more advanced players will fake a smash and barely drop the ball over the net if the opponent is deep in the backcourt and expecting a hard smash. Until you become adept in executing the hard, fast smash, it is better to achieve good placement and accuracy.

## THE CHOP

This stroke consists of "chopping" down and underneath the ball so as to give it backspin, resulting in a low, short bounce. The grip is the same as used in the forehand or the backhand drive, and the racket head is above the wrist, which is locked upon contact with the ball. This shot is used defensively to return an opponent's hard serve or offensive shot, or to slow down the pace of the rally (Illus. 35, 36, 37).

Offensively, you may use it to capture points by dropping balls barely over the net with a stroke referred to as the "drop shot."

Reserved specifically for more advanced players, the drop shot can be very effective when executed correctly and deceptively. The drop shot leaves the opponent playing in the backcourt flat-footed and unable to reach the ball in time. The forehand or backhand grip is used as necessary, and the backswing is the same as in the forehand or backhand drive, except slightly higher. A downward motion is made to impart backspin, and the follow-through stops almost immediately after contact with the ball. This shot is difficult to execute with any real degree of accuracy and should not be made from farther back than the service line.

*Illustration 35*
*Forehand chop*
*backswing*

*Illustration 36*
*Forehand chop*
*contact*

*Illustration 37*
*Forehand chop*
*follow-through*

## THE SLICE

The difference between the chop and the slice is that in the slice there is sidespin on the ball imparted by much wrist action. Swing the racket down and to the far side of the ball to make it bounce low and off to one side. The follow-through is longer than in the chop and is finished in a downward rather than an upward motion.

## SUGGESTIONS FOR BEGINNERS

1. Be certain to take the proper backswing, and pivot with the side to the net when executing ground strokes.

2. Hit the ball straight through, waist high, with a flat racket, and

shift the weight forward into the shot.

3. Follow through with a free, easy swing in the direction in which the ball should go, and swing the racket slightly up and around.

4. Keep eyes on the ball. Hit the ball in the center of the racket.

5. Remember that control and accuracy are more important than power and speed.

6. Bend from the knees and waist to get down to the height of the ball. Do not drop the racket head below wrist level.

7. Take balls at the height of their bounce except for shoulder-high balls, which are often better handled when allowed to drop to waist-high position.

8. Aim several feet above the net to cut down on the possibility of hitting the ball into the net.

9. Make more cross-court than down-the-line shots, since the net is 6 inches lower in the middle than at the sides.

## PLAYING STRATEGY

1. Keep ball in play until the opportunity for a placement arises.

2. Hit the ball deep to keep the opponent on the defensive.

3. Return to home base position after making each shot, except when rushing the net.

4. Play to the opponent's weakness, but don't overdo it. Sometimes through constant attack the weakness becomes strength.

5. Vary placements and pace of the ball. Keep the opponent guessing.

6. Be alert to anticipate opponent's returns. Think ahead, planning your own strategy as you play.

7. Take your time, and relax.

8. Play just one point at a time. Always control your temper.

9. Never change tactics when you are winning, but figure out different strategy when losing.

10. Expect to win, and *never give up!*

## THE DOUBLES GAME

The doubles game is very much different from the singles game. It is amazing to discover that the outstanding singles players are not always the best doubles players. Likewise, the best doubles players are not

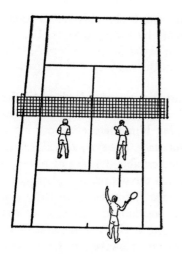

*Illustration 38*
*Doubles serving and net positions*

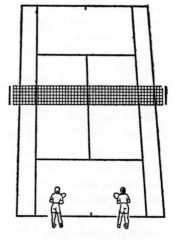

*Illustration 39*
*Doubles backcourt position*

always good singles players. Besides there being four players in doubles, and the doubles court being 9 feet wider than the singles court, there are essential differences in the game itself, which are

> 1. Singles play is more a base line battle, with occasional net rushes and placements. In doubles play, net exchanges are much more frequent, with few points being scored from the backcourt. This makes doubles a faster game than singles.
>
> 2. Singles depends on individual effort; doubles, on teamwork.
>
> 3. In singles play, ground strokes are more prevalent. In doubles, the volley, smash, and lob assume greater importance.
>
> 4. The serve in singles is usually harder. In doubles, it is more important to have a slower serve with spin and placement to allow the server to gain the net position.

Partners in doubles always play side by side, rather than up and back. In other words, both players cover the length of their own individual sides of the court rather than the width of the court. The server's partner plays at the net, and the server should follow his serve up to the net to maintain a parallel position (Illus. 38). If the opponents lob over their heads, the net players retreat together to a parallel position in the backcourt (Illus. 39). They play in this position until they have opportunity to regain the net and attempt to put the ball away.

Players should never play one up and one back. This action leaves too many vulnerable spots for placements by the opponents. For example, the opponents can hit a ball to the player in the backcourt, then rush the net and volley the return between the net man and his partner (Illus. 40).

When receiving in doubles, both partners can play back until the opportunity to move in, or the nonreceiving partner can play the net position, anticipating his partner's joining him there after making a good, low service return (Illus. 41). Sometimes, however, a weak return of service places the net partner in the undesirable position of having a ball volleyed directly at him. For this reason the nonreceiver playing net should stand about a step inside the service line rather than the usual closer net position. From this modified position the net partner can move back or at least be able to cover more territory in defense of an attempted putaway shot by the opponents. However, if the service return is an effective one, the net partner moves on toward the normal attacking net position, about four or five feet from the net.

*Illustration 40*
*Poor doubles playing position*

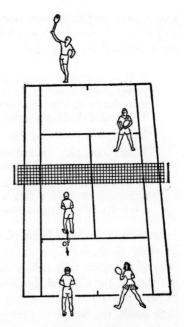

*Illustration 41*
*Doubles receiving position*

## DOUBLES PLAY TACTICS

1. Hit the ball deep to the center of the court. This leaves no possibility of sharply angled returns, and often confuses the opponents over which partner should play the ball.

2. Get the first serve in the court, and advance to the net position.

3. Stay in a position parallel with your partner, either at the net or in the backcourt.

4. Make low returns of your opponent's serves so that they will have to "volley up."

5. Call "yours" or "mine" when it is doubtful which partner should make the return. When a ball goes between two partners, the person with the forehand should take the ball.

6. Cover partner's area when he is drawn out of court making a return.

7. Play to the weakness of either or both opponents.

8. Develop a good lob, smash, and volley.

9. Make use of the lob to drive the opponents away from the net.

10. Hit the ball down between the opponents or at their feet when at the net with them.

11. Be alert and cooperate with partner at all times.

# RULES

### Court (Rule 1)*

The dimensions of the tennis court for singles and doubles are as shown in Illustration 4, page 11.

### Server and Receiver (Rule 4)

The "server" puts the ball into play, and the "receiver" is his opponent.

### Choice of Sides or Service (Rule 5)

1. The winner of the toss has the choice of
   a. Serving or receiving.
   b. Side of court.
2. The toss is made by placing the head of the racket on the court and spinning it. As it spins, the opponent calls some differentiating characteristic on the racket, such as roughness or smoothness of the trim at the top and bottom of the racket head or a trademark.

### Service Delivery (Rules 6, 8, 10)

1. Before the server begins to serve, he must stand with both feet behind the base line within imaginary extensions of the center mark and side line.
2. The service always begins to the right of the center mark and is made to the opponent's right service court. After each point is played, service courts are changed for the next service in alternating fashion.
3. The server has two service attempts to put the ball into play.
4. The serve is made by tossing the ball into the air and hitting it with the racket before it touches the ground.
5. The ball must clear the net and land in the proper service court or on one of the lines of the proper service court before being hit by the receiver. However, after the service the ball may be hit before it bounces.

* For official rules consult the "Rules of Lawn Tennis" by the USLTA, 51 E. 42nd St., New York, N.Y. 10017.

### Foot Fault (Rule 7)

1. During the delivery of the service, the server must not

   a. Change his position by walking or running.

   b. Touch with either foot any area other than that behind the base line within imaginary extensions of center mark and side line.

2. The rear foot may swing over the base line before the ball is struck if it does not touch the court.

### Faults (Rule 9)

1. The service is a fault if the server

   a. Does not take the proper position before serving.

   b. Commits a foot fault.

   c. Misses the ball in attempting to strike it. However, the server may toss and catch the ball without penalty.

   d. Fails to hit the ball into the proper service court.

   e. Serves the ball so that it hits a permanent structure other than the net, strap, or band.

   f. Hits his partner or anything he wears or carries with the served ball.

2. If any of these occurs on the first service, it is a single fault.

3. If any of these occurs on both services, it is a double fault and the point is lost.

### The Let (Rule 12)

1. A let is a ball which on service touches the net, strap, or band and is otherwise good.

2. A let is called when a player is unable to play a shot due to circumstances beyond his control, such as interference by a ball or a player from another court.

3. A let also occurs if a service is delivered before the receiver is ready. If, however, the receiver attempts to return the service, he is considered to be ready.

4. When a let occurs on a service, only that service is repeated; if it occurs during play, the point is replayed (this allows two services).

### Player Loses Point (Rules 16, 17, 18)

A player loses the point if

1. The ball bounces twice on his side of the net or if he does not return the ball to his opponent's court.
2. His body, clothing, or racket touch the net while the ball is in play.
3. He reaches over the net to play a ball unless the ball has bounced back over the net due to spin or the wind.
4. The ball strikes him during play even if he is out-of-bounds.
5. He throws the racket at the ball and makes an otherwise good return.
6. He hits the ball more than once. In doubles the ball may be returned by only one partner.

### Good Returns (Rule 22)

It is a good return if

1. The ball lands on any boundary line.
2. The ball touches the top of a net post or the net and falls into the proper court.
3. A player goes beyond the net post to play a ball and successfully returns it outside the post, either above or below the net height.
4. A player follows through over the net but does not touch the net.

### Scoring (Rules 24, 25)

1. The server's score is always called first.
2. The score in tennis is 15 for the first point won, 30 for the second, 40 for the third point, and "game" for the fourth point won. A score of zero is referred to as "love." When each side has a score of 40, the score is "deuce," which means that one side must win two consecutive points in order to win the game. If the server wins the next point, the score is called "advantage in" and if he wins the following point it is game. If the receiver wins the first point after deuce, the score is called "advantage out" and if he wins the next point it is his game. However, if, after the score is either advantage in or advantage out, the other player wins the next point, the score then becomes deuce again.
3. The side reaching six games first wins the "set" unless the score is five games apiece, called a "deuce set," in which case one side must gain a two-game lead to win the set. Two out of three sets constitutes a "match"; however, in some tournaments men play three out of five sets.

## Changing Sides (Rule 26)

The players change sides of court at the end of the first, third, and every subsequent alternate game of each set, and at the end of each set —unless the total number of games in such a set is even, in which case the change is not made until the end of the first game of the next set.

### Serving in Doubles (Rules 33, 35)

1. The order of serving is decided at the beginning of each set. The pair serving first decides who is to serve in the first game, and the other partner will serve in the third game. The opponents also decide who is to serve first in the second game, and the other partner will serve in the fourth game. Both pairs alternate in the remaining games of the set.

2. The server's partner may stand anywhere during service, but he usually stands within eight feet of the net and in a position so that he can cover his half of the court.

3. If a player serves out of turn, the proper server must serve as soon as the mistake is discovered. All points earned are counted. If a complete game is played with the wrong server, the order of service remains as altered.

### Receiving in Doubles (Rules 34, 36)

1. The order of receiving is decided at the beginning of each set. The pair receiving in the first game decide who will receive first, and that player will continue to receive first in all odd-numbered games of the set. The opponents will also decide who will receive first in the second game, and he will receive the first service in all even-numbered games of the set. Players alternate receiving services during a game.

2. If a player receives out of turn, he remains in that position until the game in which it is discovered is completed. The partners then resume their original positions.

## SOME *DO'S* AND *DON'TS* OF TENNIS

**DO:**

1. Retrieve your ball from another court only when play on that court is completed. If convenient, politely ask players on that court to return it.

2. Return balls from other courts by rolling them to the players or

to the fence behind their court if they are playing.

3. Call a let when there is interference during play or when a ball lands so close to a line that it is difficult to determine whether or not it is good.

4. Collect all balls on your side of the net after each point and return them to the server.

5. Recognize a good play by your partner or your opponent.

6. Display good sportsmanship when winning or losing.

7. Play doubles rather than singles when others are waiting, and play only a set.

## DON'T:

1. Walk behind a court while play is in progress.

2. Hesitate in calling services "good" or "out" on those that land near the boundary of the service court.

3. Return or retrieve first services that are not good. The server should not be interrupted while serving.

4. Delay play by retrieving balls slowly, or by conversing with passers-by.

5. Criticize your partner or try to play the whole court yourself.

6. Talk loudly near a match.

7. Practice or warm up near a court while playing is going on, or play on adjacent courts during tournament competition.

8. Try to coach or officiate a match unless acting in that capacity.

9. Play on clay or dirt courts when they are soft from rain. Footprints and holes are difficult to repair after the court dries.

# SELF-IMPROVEMENT AND TRAINING

An avid tennis player improves his skill and physical fitness through a daily schedule of practice, play, and exercise. A person cannot expect to become a great tennis player, even with natural ability, unless he is willing to set up a training program. The program, however, can be worthwhile in this task only to the extent that a player believes in it and has a sincere willingness to follow it. The main purposes of a program are to develop (1) skill, (2) physical fitness, and (3) health habits.

## DEVELOPMENT OF SKILL

Beginners must first learn the proper technique in executing fundamentals. This information is contained in Chapter 4. After understanding how to execute a stroke, do it many times to establish correct habits. As an aid to accomplishing these correct habits, a list of "Skills Tests" and "Tennis Improvement Charts" are presented in Chapter 8. Although these aids are designed to help you master the basic fundamentals, the real proof lies in how well you can apply them to the actual game situation. This demands self-discipline and concentrated effort. Improvement and perfection in executing strokes can be accomplished only through proper stroke technique. You may get the ball over the net by using your own poor technique, but you will probably not improve to any great extent or become a very good player. It is most important, then, that you learn proper techniques and diligently practice and play using them.

The player with an intermediate or advanced level of skill approaches skill development in a slightly different way. The knowledge of how to execute the various strokes has been acquired. However, because of the variety of strokes in tennis, one, two, or maybe all the strokes will need additional emphasis through practice. It is also necessary to continue to practice all skills of the game to maintain or increase proficiency in the strokes of tennis. The following procedures can be used:

1. Practice "stroking" test for intermediate-to-advanced players listed in Chapter 8.

2. Hit against a practice board or wall with a line marked across it at correct net level. Work for consistency and accuracy.

3. Use an automatic ball-tossing machine and practice hitting the following shots.

    a. Forehands and backhands (cross-court and down-the-line)

    b. Forehand and backhand volleys (drop-volleys included)

    c. Lobs and smashes

    d. Drop-shots executed from about the service line rather than from the baseline

    e. Occasional half-volleys, chops, and slices

4. Practice with a partner.

    a. Serve and practice service returns. Serve to forehand and backhand side of receiver who practices cross-court and down-the-line returns. Practice using chop shots to return hard, fast serves when necessary. Alternate positions and serve at least twenty to twenty-five balls each.

    b. Alternate practice of lobs and smashes. Do at least fifteen of each.

    c. Volley back and forth. Start near the service line and slowly move closer to the net. Use forehand and backhand volley strokes. Hit for at least 3–5 minutes.

    d. Alternate hitting drives across net to partner, who makes returns using a chop or slice stroke. Drill on both forehand and backhand strokes and hit at least twenty-five each.

5. Practice the service by yourself. Use a bucket of balls on an empty court, and serve over and over again. Practice placements to both forehand and backhand corners of both service courts.

6. Play some games using one type of stroke only to score points; that is, only shots made with a backhand, or a smash, or a volley can score points.

7. Play points only and don't keep game score. Concentrate on proper execution and placement, and practice weak strokes.

8. Keep a record of a specific number of successful tries using various strokes.

9. Practice placement of the various strokes by marking off areas of the court using chalk, towels, or "punching clowns."

10. Use a suspended ball or tethered ball and practice strokes that can make use of the position of the ball. Concentrate on form and footwork.

11. Leave each practice with a desire to play some more. This keeps enthusiasm high and prevents practice from being a drudgery.

## DEVELOPMENT OF PHYSICAL FITNESS

One difficulty of many students in learning tennis is the lack of physical fitness. This makes basic movements more difficult because they haven't adequate strength to hold or swing the racket properly, or sufficient endurance to move repeatedly to hit the ball.

Developing physical fitness involves exercising in addition to practicing or playing tennis. The body improves only to the point of the demand put upon it. A beginner does not put very much demand upon the body in practice or play because much of the time is spent in retrieving balls. Thus other exercises must be done.

The part of the training program involving exercise should not take long. A well-rounded series of exercises lasting from 5 to 10 minutes should be sufficient for the beginner or intermediate player. Those who are planning a competitive schedule, however, will want to do more than ten minutes of exercise in order to develop a higher level of endurance. Exercises should involve the hands, arms, shoulders, trunk, and legs. Strength, endurance, and flexibility must be established and maintained.

Exercises to develop and increase strength and endurance of the grip, arm, and shoulder can be selected from the following:

1. Squeeze a rubber ball, or an old tennis ball, or any kind of rubber or spongy material that will fit into the hand and allow the fingers to close over it. (Grip)

2. Squeeze hands with a partner. (Grip)

3. Tighten and loosen the forehand and backhand grips on the racket. (Grip)

4. Grasp hand of partner with one foot parallel and touching one foot of his and attempt to move him off balance—Indian wrestling. (Grip and arm)

5. Bounce a ball on the court and in the air with the press on the racket. Use both forehand and backhand grips. (Grip, arm and shoulder)

6. Hold racket, with press on, in various positions for a 10-second count in each position. Some of the positions are: (a) horizontally sideward, (b) horizontally forward, (c) horizontally backward. The body should remain in an upright position. (Arm and shoulder)

7. Do push-ups with the body straight from head to feet with hands and toes on the ground, or with the body straight from head to knees with the hands and knees on the ground. A large

number of repetitions is not needed, but being able to do from five to ten push-ups will be beneficial. (Arm and shoulder)

8. Throw a softball with an overhand motion. (Arm and shoulder; also aids development of serve coordination)

Exercises to develop the trunk and legs can be selected from the following:

1. Rotate the trunk. Assume a standing position, feet shoulder-width apart, and hands clasped behind the head. Bend forward and then rotate clockwise bending as far as possible. Do this five times and then rotate counterclockwise five times. (Increases trunk flexibility)

2. Touch the fists to the toes with legs straight. Do at least ten times. (Increases back and leg flexibility)

3. Do sit-ups with legs bent and hands clasped behind the head. By bending the legs and placing the feet flat on the ground, the abdominal muscles will have a greater stress put upon them. Do at least ten and increase to twenty-five.(Strengthens abdominal muscles and increases trunk flexibility)

4. Lunge forward from a standing position with arms extended sideward. Place right foot 18 to 30 inches forward, bend right leg, lean forward until chest touches thigh, and wrap arms around upper leg just above knee and squeeze. Return to standing position and repeat with left foot forward. Start with at least five repetitions with each leg and increase. (Increases leg strength and trunk flexibility)

5. Jump and reach. Starting position is with the legs bent, body in a semi-crouching position, arms extended backward. Swing arms forward and upward and jump upward. Swing arms downward when landing and as arms swing backward make a short jump with both feet. Repeat at least ten times and increase to twenty times. (Good as a warm-up exercise, helps develop some strength and endurance of the legs, and helps improve coordination)

6. Do standing broad jumps. Start with ten jumps and increase to twenty. (Helps develop leg strength and endurance)

7. Run 30- or 40-yard sprints. Start with three and increase. (Develops quickness of movement and helps build leg strength)

8. Run 20-yard sprints backward. Start with three and increase. (Develops leg strength and coordination)

9. Jump rope. Start slowly, increase speed, and exercise for 1 minute. Increase length of time for exercising. Also jump by alternating the speed—slow, fast, medium, fast, slow. (Develops coordination, leg strength, and endurance)

10. Do a boxer's footwork drill, which involves forward and backward running and side-stepping to both sides. Do not cross the legs. Start with a 2-minute drill and increase the length of time. (Develops coordination and speed of movement and leg strength and endurance)

11. Do three-quarter knee bends. Start with fifteen and increase to at least twenty-five. (Develops leg strength and flexibility)

12. Run 50 yards with a person of equal weight on the back. For girls, and boys with very weak legs, this should be eliminated or done with a person weighing less than their weight. (Develops leg strength and endurance)

## DEVELOPMENT OF HEALTH HABITS

Progress in skill and physical fitness depends to a great extent on proper body care. It is a necessity as higher levels of training are followed. Once again, knowing what to do is but one part of the process; application of such knowledge is equally important.

The following habits should be developed:

1. Exercise regularly several times a week. If tennis is not played, another vigorous game should be played in addition to regular conditioning exercises.

2. Eat a well-balanced diet with emphasis on green vegetables and proteins. Eat at regular hours each day and do not eat between meals. Eating snacks tends to reduce the appetite with the result that the snacks may replace more vital items in the diet.

3. Do not eat immediately after strenuous exercise. Allow the body time to cool off and body functions time to return to normal.

4. Drink at least six glasses of water a day. Drinking cool liquids during and after strenuous exercise will help reduce body temperature.

5. Do not drink alcoholic beverages of any kind.

6. Shower immediately after practice or workout. Do not sit or lie around in damp clothes. Use soap and hot water to clean all parts of the body thoroughly.

7. Wear clean clothes not only for appearance, but also to help prevent skin irritations and infections.

8. Wear a sweater or jacket after playing to prevent colds or sore muscles.

9. Obtain at least 8 hours of sleep every night. Regular hours are more beneficial to the body than just a set number of hours.

10. Keep a balance in life by not overdoing any one phase of it. Take time to develop the physical, mental, social, and spiritual sides of life.

# GLOSSARY

*Ace:* Good service that is not touched by the opponent.

*"Ad":* Abbreviation for advantage.

*Advantage:* Next point after deuce. "Advantage in" refers to the server's winning the point, and "advantage out" refers to the receiver's winning the point.

*All:* Tie score. This is used when deuce is not applicable, such as "30 all."

*Alley:* Area between the singles side line and the side line on a doubles court.

*Backcourt:* Area of the court between the service line and the base line. This area is commonly known as "No Man's Land."

*Backhand:* Stroke used to hit balls on the left side of a right-handed player and on the right side of a left-handed player.

*Backspin:* Rotation of the ball so that the top of the ball spins backward.

*Base line:* Line at each end of the court.

*Break a serve:* Phrase used to indicate winning a game that the opponent served.

*Center mark:* Mark four inches long and two inches wide that bisects the base line to indicate one limit of the proper service area.

*Center service line:* Line down the center of the court that separates the service courts.

*Center strap:* Two-inch-wide piece of canvas that holds the net down at the center.

*Chop:* Stroke in which the racket is drawn sharply down under the ball to give it backspin.

*Cross-court:* Phrase indicating a ball hit diagonally from one corner across the net to another corner.

*Deep:* Term referring to a shot that lands near the base line.

*Deuce:* Even score when each side has won three or more points.

*Double fault:* Failure on two consecutive services.

*Down-the-line*: Phrase indicating ball hit straight across the net to the opposite court near the side line.

*Doubles*: Play with two persons on each side.

*Drive*: Shot hit hard without much of an arc so that it lands near the opponent's base line.

*Drop shot*: Shot hit easily with backspin so that it barely clears the net and does not bounce very high in the opponent's court.

*Error*: Failure to make a legal return when racket has hit the ball.

*Fault*: Failure to make a legal service.

*Flat*: Shot or serve with little or no spin.

*Foot fault*: Illegal movement of the feet during service.

*Forcing shot*: Deep, hard shot designed to maneuver an opponent out of position.

*Forecourt*: Area of the court between the net and the service line.

*Forehand*: Stroke used to hit balls on the right side of a right-handed player and on the left side of a left-handed player.

*Game*: Unit of a set completed by winning four points before opponent wins three, or by winning two consecutive points after deuce.

*Good*: Shot that lands on or within the proper boundary lines.

*Ground stroke*: Stroke made by hitting the ball after it has bounced.

*Half-volley*: Stroke made by hitting the ball immediately after it has hit the ground.

*Kill*: Hard-hit or well-placed ball that the opponent cannot reach for a return.

*Let*: Service or point that is to be replayed because of some type of interference.

*Lob*: Shot with a high arc so that it lands near the opponent's base line.

*Love*: Zero score.

*Match*: Contest between two or four players usually consisting of two out of three sets.

*Match point*: Point that, if won, allows a player to win the match.

*Mixed doubles*: Game in which a man and a woman play as partners on each side.

*Net man*: Player in doubles who plays near the net while his partner serves or receives.

*Overhead smash:* Shot made with a hard overhead stroke so that the ball comes down sharply into the opponent's court. This shot is usually referred to as the "smash."

*Pass:* Shot going to either side of an opponent near the net out of his reach.

*Placement:* Shot placed accurately out of the reach of the opponent.

*Rally:* Continued play between the serve and the winning of a point.

*Seeding:* Placing of good players in tournament competition so that they do not meet in early round play.

*Service:* Putting the ball into play.

*Set:* Unit of a match completed by winning six games, or by winning two consecutive games after each side has won five games.

*Set point:* Point that, if won, allows a player to win the set.

*Side line:* Lines on each side of the court. The singles side line is the boundary for singles play, while the doubles side line is the boundary for doubles play.

*Singles:* Play with one person on each side of the net.

*Slice:* Stroke in which the racket is drawn sharply down across the ball with wrist action to give sidespin.

*Take the net:* Player rushes to a position close to the net to volley.

*Tape:* Two- to two-and-one-half-inch piece of canvas that covers the cord or cable at the top of the net.

*Topspin:* Rotation of the ball so that the top of the ball spins forward.

*Toss:* The spin of the racket at the beginning of a match to determine choice of serving or receiving, or side of court.

*Trim:* Small stringing at top and bottom of racket head to hold the main strings in place. This stringing is used in the toss to indicate "rough" or "smooth." The rough side contains the loops around the main strings while the smooth is the opposite side.

*Volley:* Ball hit in the air before it bounces.

*Wide:* Shot that lands beyond the side line.

# SELF-TESTING AND EVALUATION

As a beginner, you should not advance too rapidly in your desire to become a highly skilled player, nor should you practice the same elementary techniques when you have sufficiently mastered them. The tests in this chapter will enable you to determine your status and regulate your future practice and study accordingly. The skills tests are arranged in a progressive order and those listed as "nonstroking" for a beginner should be mastered before moving to the "stroking" tests. A certain number of repetitions is listed for each test, and the ability to do the number listed, in the manner listed, indicates mastery.

## SKILLS TESTS

The following are "nonstroking" tests designed to develop coordination, grip strength, and endurance.

1. Bounce ball on floor with racket, using forehand and backhand grips. Do each 100 times consecutively.

2. Bounce ball into air with racket. Do 50 times consecutively.

3. Toss ball into air and catch on racket. Be successful eight out of ten tries.

4. Catch ball on racket after a bounce from a toss by partner. Be successful eight out of ten tries.

5. Bounce ball on floor and then bounce ball into air. Alternate ten down and ten up until 100 is reached.

The following are "stroking" tests for beginners to develop proficiency in playing skills.

1. Bounce and hit ball over net.
   a. Forehand and backhand drives from base line. Be successful fifteen out of twenty times.
   b. Forehand and backhand cross-court shots from the base line. Be successful fifteen out of twenty times.
   c. Forehand and backhand down-the-line-shots from the base line. Be successful fifteen out of twenty times.

2. Hit ball against backboard or wall. Forehand and backhand drives. Do each ten times consecutively.

3. Serve the ball into the right and left service courts. Be successful five out of ten tries in each court.

The following are "stroking" tests for intermediate-to-advanced players to develop more advanced skills in stroking.

1. Bounce and hit ball over net into singles court area. Use forehand and backhand drives. Be successful fifteen out of twenty tries.

2. Bounce and hit ball over net to cross-court corner. Use forehand drive from forehand corner and backhand drive from backhand corner. Be successful on fifteen out of twenty tries.

3. Bounce and hit ball over the net and down the line with the forehand drive from the forehand corner and with the backhand drive from the backhand corner. Be successful on fifteen out of twenty tries.

4. Bounce and hit forehand and backhand lob shots from base line to base line. Be successful on fifteen out of twenty tries.

5. Use a toss by partner or a ball-throwing machine to
   a. Repeat numbers, *1, 2, 3*, and *4* above.
   b. Hit forehand and backhand volley shots across net. Be successful fifteen out of twenty tries.
   c. Hit overhead smash shots into other court. Be successful on fifteen out of twenty tries.
   d. Hit chop and slice strokes across net. Be successful on fifteen out of twenty tries in each stroke.

6. Hit ball against backboard or wall. Use forehand and backhand drives and do each fifteen times consecutively.

7. Serve the ball into the right and left service courts. Be successful on fifteen out of twenty serves into each court.

The "Tennis Improvement Chart for Beginners" (Chart A) should be used to record progress on the "nonstroking" and "stroking" skills tests for beginners. Each test is listed with space to record at least four trials. After instruction and practice in an area, take the appropriate test and record the result under "First Trial." After more practice, if necessary, repeat the test and record the result under "Second Trial," and so forth. When the number of tries has been attained as suggested in the test, go to the next test. "Tennis Improvement Chart for Intermediate-to-Advanced Players," (Chart B) is to be used for recording the trials on the "stroking" skills tests for intermediate-to-advanced players.

## CHART A

| TEST ITEMS | First Trial | Second Trial | Third Trial | Fourth Trial |
|---|---|---|---|---|
| Consecutive forehand bounces, 100 times | | | | |
| Consecutive backhand bounces, 100 times | | | | |
| Consecutive air bounces, 50 times | | | | |
| Toss & catch—racket, 10 tries | | | | |
| Partner toss; catch—racket, 10 tries | | | | |
| Consecutive bounces—floor-air, 100 times | | | | |
| Bounce & hit over net, 20 tries each | | | | |
| Forehand drives | | | | |
| Backhand drives | | | | |
| Forehand cross-court | | | | |
| Backhand cross-court | | | | |
| Forehand drive down-the-line | | | | |
| Backhand drive down-the-line | | | | |
| Consecutive forehand drives— wall, 10 times | | | | |
| Consecutive backhand drives— wall, 10 times | | | | |
| Serve—right court, 10 tries | | | | |
| Serve—left court, 10 tries | | | | |

## CHART B

| . TEST ITEMS | First Trial | Second Trial | Third Trial | Fourth Trial |
|---|---|---|---|---|
| Bounce & hit over net, 20 tries each<br>Forehand drive into singles court | | | | |
| Backhand drive into singles court | | | | |
| Forehand cross-court into court | | | | |
| Backhand cross-court into court | | | | |
| Forehand drive down-the-line | | | | |
| Backhand drive down-the-line | | | | |
| Forehand lob shot | | | | |
| Backhand lob shot | | | | |
| From toss or machine, 20 tries each<br>Forehand drive into singles court | | | | |
| Backhand drive into singles court | | | | |
| Forehand cross-court into court | | | | |
| Backhand cross-court into court | | | | |
| Forehand drive down-the-line | | | | |
| Backhand drive down-the-line | | | | |
| Forehand lob shot | | | | |
| Backhand lob shot | | | | |
| Forehand volley | | | | |
| Backhand volley | | | | |
| Chop stroke | | | | |
| Slice stroke | | | | |
| Consecutive forehand drive—wall;<br>15 times | | | | |
| Consecutive backhand drive—wall,<br>15 times | | | | |
| Serve—right court, 20 tries | | | | |
| Serve—left court, 20 tries | | | | |

## WRITTEN TEST

A knowledge of tennis leads to a better understanding and an increased appreciation of it. Both are important to the player and to the spectator. The following knowledge test covers the content of the preceding chapters and should be used to assist in determining how well the material has been learned. The questions are best used as a test after reading and studying, rather than as a guide on what to read in the chapters in order to answer the questions. The following scale indicates the degree of success on the test: *Excellent,* 46–50 correct; *Good,* 41–45 correct; *Average,* 36–40 correct; *Poor,* 31–35 correct; *Very Poor;* 30 and below.

### *MULTIPLE-CHOICE ITEMS*

Select the *one* best answer and circle the letter of the answer. (Answer sheets or a sheet of paper properly numbered may be used.)

1. Which of the following scores would indicate that the set was complete?
   *a.* 5–1  *b.* 6–5  *c.* 8–6  *d.* 9–8

2. What is the minimum number of points that must be played in order to win a game?
   *a.* 3  *b.* 4  *c.* 5  *d.* 6

3. Which of these scores would be called "deuce"?
   *a.* Each team has two points  *b.* Each team has three points
   *c.* Each team has the same number of points  *d.* One team has two points and the other team has three points

4. What is the term that designates a point that must be replayed?
   *a.* net ball  *b.* let  *c.* dead ball  *d.* fault

5. What is the correct position of the thumb on the forehand grip?
   *a.* around the handle  *b.* extended straight up the handle
   *c.* extended diagonally around the handle  *d.* held next to the index finger

6. Which forehand grip can best be used for hitting high or low bouncing balls with maximum support from the wrist?
   *a.* Western  *b.* Eastern  *c.* Continental  *d.* Modified Western

7. Which of the following best describes the body position for the forehand drive?
   *a.* facing the net  *b.* facing the side line  *c.* standing at a 45-degree

angle to the net   *d.* standing at a 135-degree angle to the net

8. When should players change sides of court? After each:
   *a.* game   *b.* set   *c.* even-numbered game   *d.* odd-numbered game

9. Which of the following indicates the best place on the court to make the overhead smash shot?
   *a.* forecourt   *b.* backcourt   *c.* service line   *d.* back line

10. What is the purpose of the lob shot?
    *a.* to speed up the play   *b.* to slow down the play   *c.* to force the opponent from the net   *d.* to give the player time to go to the net

11. What effect does hitting a tennis ball with backspin have on the bounce of the ball? Makes the:
    *a.* bounce lower   *b.* bounce higher   *c.* angle of the bounce greater   *d.* speed of the bounce greater

12. Where is the best place to wait for the ball during a rally in singles? Center of the:
    *a.* court   *b.* base line   *c.* service line   *d.* backcourt

13. What is the meaning of the term "ace"?
    *a.* the server won the point   *b.* first ball on the service was a good serve   *c.* receiver was unable to return the service   *d.* receiver was unable to contact the first ball of the service

14. What is the difference in width between the doubles and the singles court in tennis?
    *a.* 7 feet   *b.* 8 feet   *c.* 9 feet   *d.* 10 feet

15. Which of the following best indicates the essentials of a good serve?
    *a.* accuracy, placement, speed   *b.* slice, spin, speed   *c.* placement, speed, rebound   *d.* placement, speed, spin

16. Which of the following is the most desirable spot for contacting the ball on the backhand drive?
    *a.* opposite the rear foot   *b.* opposite the forward foot   *c.* just ahead of the rear foot   *d.* just behind the forward foot

17. Which of the following will have the greatest speed if other things are equal? A ball hit with:
    *a.* backspin   *b.* topspin   *c.* no spin   *d.* sidespin

18. What kind of wood is used in the best grade of tennis racket frames?
    *a.* ash   *b.* hickory   *c.* hard maple   *d.* hard pine

19. What should be the umpire's decision if the receiver returns a ball which passes outside the net post below the level of the top of the net and then falls inside the server's court?
    *a.* let ball   *b.* ball in play   *c.* point awarded server   *d.* point awarded receiver

20. What would usually be the most advantageous stroke to use against the short lob?
    *a.* chop   *b.* smash   *c.* drop   *d.* deep lob

21. Which of the following indicates the type of opponent it is advisable to use a drop shot against? One who:
    *a.* is skilled at volleying   *b.* goes to the net frequently   *c.* prefers to play at the base line   *d.* likes to use a chop stroke

22. What is the decision of the umpire in a singles game if the server delivers the second ball of a service while standing behind the base line back of the alley and the serve lands in the proper court?
    *a.* ball in play   *b.* ball is re-served   *c.* point awarded server   *d.* point awarded receiver

23. What should be the umpire's decision if a player serves, loses the point, and then it was discovered that the serve was made from the wrong court?
    *a.* declare a let   *b.* award point to server   *c.* award point to receiver   *d.* order ball re-served from correct court

24. What is the most probable cause if a player consistently sends balls too far to the left in executing the backhand drive?
    *a.* body facing the net   *b.* insufficient force on the swing   *c.* forward swing made too late   *d.* forward swing taken too early

25. What is the score when the server wins the next point after deuce?
    *a.* game   *b.* 40–30   *c.* advantage in   *d.* advantage out

26. What is the relationship of the racket face to the ground when executing a forehand drive on a ball bouncing waist high?
    *a.* parallel   *b.* perpendicular   *c.* slanted forward   *d.* slanted backward

27. Which of the following governs the play of tennis in this country?
    *a.* United States Tennis Association   *b.* United States Lawn Tennis Association   *c.* American Tennis Association   *d.* American Lawn Tennis Association

28. Which country gave rise to the game of tennis as we know it today?
    *a.* France   *b.* England   *c.* Bermuda   *d.* United States

29. When should the body weight be transferred forward on drives?
    *a.* at time ball is contacted   *b.* just before ball is contacted   *c.* just

after ball is contacted   *d.* as soon as forward swing is started
30. Where are the World Amateur Tennis Championships held?
    *a.* Forest Hills, N.Y.   *b.* Wimbledon, England   *c.* Sydney, Australia   *d.* Paris, France

## TRUE-FALSE ITEMS

Mark "T" if the statement is true; mark "F" if the statement is false. (Answer sheets or a sheet of paper properly numbered may be used.)
31. A deep service is used to prevent the receiver from coming to the net.
32. In getting into position to meet the ball, moderately long steps are preferable to short ones.
33. The server may jump into the air as he serves the ball.
34. A short stroke with a wrist snap is recommended for all ground strokes.
35. A strategic placement for a cross-court shot is the spot where the service line and side line meet.
36. A beginner should attempt to receive the serve on the forehand side.
37. Beginners should try to clear the net by 1–3 feet on every drive.
38. In doubles, the order of serving established at the beginning of a match must be maintained throughout the match.
39. A deep, high lob shot sets up an easy return for an opponent.
40. It is more important in doubles than in singles that the first ball of the service be good.
41. The half-volley is used on balls that hit near the feet.
42. It is possible for a player to lose games by consistently playing to an opponent's weakness.
43. A player intending to volley should get as close to the net as possible.
44. It is legal to serve with an underhand motion.
45. A player loses the game if after he has gained "advantage point" his opponent wins two consecutive points.
46. If on the serve the receiver is not ready but makes an attempt to return the ball and fails, the point is played over.
47. The server serves from the left court when the score is 40–30.
48. A volley is a series of legal returns during play.
49. A player loses the point if he reaches over the net to hit the ball be-before it has crossed over the net.
50. Tennis was introduced into the United States during the first half of the nineteenth century.

## RATING SCALES

A rating is a subjective estimate of performance, and is used to deter-mine the mastery of skill in areas where there are no specific objective tests or in areas where tests do not measure actual game situations. The rating in tennis is used to evaluate performance during play or practice; therefore, it must be done by an observer. This person should have a thorough knowledge of the area being rated in order to determine the degree of proficiency of the performer.

The rating scale in Chart C is used to indicate over-all tennis ability and is a *general* rating scale. This scale is used for evaluation of players during actual play and is a convenient way to compare performance of members of a class or group. The rating scale in Chart D is used to indicate ability in the specific phases of each stroke and is a *specific* rating scale for individual players. It would be used for evaluation of players during stroke practice and could be used during actual play.

### CHART C

### TENNIS RATING SHEET

Rating scale:

1—Very poor  2—Poor  3—Average  4—Good  5—Excellent

| Name | Form | Strategy | Maneu-verability | Total Points |
|------|------|----------|------------------|--------------|
|      |      |          |                  |              |
|      |      |          |                  |              |
|      |      |          |                  |              |
|      |      |          |                  |              |
|      |      |          |                  |              |
|      |      |          |                  |              |
|      |      |          |                  |              |
|      |      |          |                  |              |
|      |      |          |                  |              |

## CHART D

### CHECKLIST FOR BASIC SKILLS IN TENNIS

Name _____

| Skill * | Ex-cellent | Good | Average | Poor | Very Poor |
|---|---|---|---|---|---|
| *Forehand drive*<br>Body position | | | | | |
| Footwork | | | | | |
| Backswing | | | | | |
| Contact with the ball | | | | | |
| Follow-through | | | | | |
| *Backhand drive*<br>Body position | | | | | |
| Footwork | | | | | |
| Backswing | | | | | |
| Contact with the ball | | | | | |
| Follow-through | | | | | |
| *Service*<br>Body position | | | | | |
| Footwork | | | | | |
| Toss of ball | | | | | |
| Backswing | | | | | |
| Contact with the ball | | | | | |
| Follow-through | | | | | |
| | | | | | |

* Additional strokes may be added.

# BIBLIOGRAPHY

**9**

## Books

Budge, J. Donald. *Budge on Tennis.* (Englewood Cliffs, N.J.: Prentice-Hall, Inc., 1939).
Budge's theory of winning tennis; fundamentals of the game; grips; mechanics of the drive, serve, smash, and volley; auxiliary strokes; psychology and strategy; doubles play; some personal tips; and a glossary of terms.

Cummings, Parke. *American Tennis.* (Boston: Little, Brown and Co., 1957).
An excellent history of the game in the United States; a listing of USLTA records; and a good bibliography of books on tennis.

Driver, Helen Irene. *Tennis for Teachers.* International Edition. (Madison, Wisconsin: Monona-Driver Book Co., 1964).
Comprehensive coverage of tennis from a brief history through equipment selection, terminology, fundamentals, tactics, games, drills, tests, lesson plans, and the organization of tennis programs and clinics. Well-illustrated with diagrams and pictures.

Kenfield, John F., Jr. *Teaching and Coaching Tennis.* (Dubuque, Iowa: William C. Brown, 1964).
A well-illustrated book covering the following areas: teaching principles, fundamentals for beginners and advanced players, group teaching techniques, aspects of coaching a team, physical care pointers, sportsmanship, and how to direct tennis tournaments.

Mottram, Tony. *Improve Your Tennis.* (Baltimore: Penguin Books, 1966).
Thoroughly covers choosing racket and equipment, mechanical fundamentals of tennis, stroke fundamentals with good pictures, footwork, spin on the ball, singles and doubles tactics, courtcraft, temperament, practicing, and conditioning, and advice to parents and juniors.

Murphy, Bill, and Murphy, Chet. *Tennis for Beginners.* (New York: Ronald Press, 1958).
A very interesting description of the game of tennis with basic rules; how to select equipment and arrange for play on a court; how to execute the forehand, backhand, serve, drive, volley, lob, overhead smash, and half-volleys; tennis strategy; doubles play; tennis manners; tournament play; practice schedule for beginners; glossary of terms.

Murphy, Bill, and Murphy, Chet. Editors. *Tennis Handbook.* (New York: Ronald Press, 1962).
An outstanding collection of articles on tennis by leading tennis players, teachers, and coaches from 1920 to 1962. The articles cover ground strokes; the serve; the volley; lesser-used shots of overhead, drop, drop-

volley, half-volley, and lob; footwork and timing; doubles; psychology, strategy, and tactics; practice and the learning process; and training and conditioning.

Talbert, William F., and Old, Bruce S. *The Game of Doubles in Tennis.* (Philadelphia: J. B. Lippincott Co., 1956).

Covers the values of tennis, short history of the game, doubles-game framework—how it should work, serve strategy, return of service, net play, base line play, and a summary. Each section is well-illustrated with play diagrams.

————. *The Game of Singles in Tennis.* (Philadelphia: J. B. Lippincott Co., 1962).

Covers the values of tennis, history of the great players, game factors for greatness, fundamentals with comprehensive discussion of placements and strategy, net play, base line play, and a summary. Each section is well-illustrated with play diagrams.

United States Lawn Tennis Association. *The Official USLTA Yearbook and Tennis Guide.* (New York: H. O. Zimman, Inc., Annual Printing).

Lists tournament schedule, officers and committees, results of previous year's cup and championship play, previous year's rankings, sectional rankings, past records, USLTA officers from 1881 to present, present membership role, constitution, by-laws, rules of the game, registry of teaching professionals, tennis foundation, and awards.

### Audio-Visual

*Basic Tennis Strokes.* (Film), 1952.[1]

Basic instruction of strokes in motion. Narrative including coaching tips accompanies action. Demonstrated by Frank Beeman. Fifteen-minute color film.

*Beginning Tennis.* (Filmstrip), 1948.[2]

The five units show history, conduct of the game, forehand and backhand drives, service, rules and etiquette.

*Fundamentals of Tennis.* (Film), 1942.[3]

The forehand and backhand drives, service, volley, half-volley, and smash are demonstrated by Don Budge.

*Slow Motion Long Films for Tennis Instruction* (Loop film).[4]

Don Budge demonstrates a different stroke in each of the six loops. Strokes are: forehand, backhand, serve, overhead smash, forehand volley, and backhand volley.

*1954 USLTA Singles Championship.* (Film).[4]

[1] Capital Film Company, East Lansing, Mich.
[2] The Athletic Institute, 209 South State Street, Chicago 4, Ill.
[3] Trans-Film, Inc., 35 West 45th St., New York 19, N.Y.
[4] United States Lawn Tennis Association, 51 E. 42nd St., New York, N.Y. 10017

Championship play of Richardson, Hoad, Hartwig, Trabert, Seixas, and Rosewall is covered, as well as a match between Doris Hart and Louise Brough.

*Tennis for Everybody.* (Film), 1960.[5]

A tennis promotion film featuring action pictures of the AAHPER-USLTA Tennis Clinic of 1,000 youngsters at the 1960 National Championships at Forest Hills, New York.

### Answers to Written Test

| | | | | | | | | |
|---|---|---|---|---|---|---|---|---|
| 1. c | 6. b | 11. a | 16. b | 21. c | 26. b | 31. T | 36. F | 41. T | 46. F |
| 2. b | 7. b | 12. b | 17. c | 22. d | 27. b | 32. F | 37. T | 42. T | 47. T |
| 3. b | 8. d | 13. d | 18. a | 23. c | 28. b | 33. T | 38. F | 43. F | 48. F |
| 4. b | 9. a | 14. c | 19. b | 24. c | 29. a | 34. F | 39. F | 44. T | 49. T |
| 5. a | 10. c | 15. d | 20. b | 25. c | 30. b | 35. T | 40. T | 45. F | 50. F |

[5] Allegro Film Productions, 723 Seventh Avenue, New York, N.Y.